Jazz: A Visual Journey
Herb Snitzer

FIRST EDITION, November, 1999

ISBN: 0-9676715-0-7

Prints and Limited Edition Collections can be purchased through:

Photograph Credits
Front Cover: *Dizzy Gillespie, New York City, 1959, Herb Snitzer - photographer*
Back Cover: *Herb Snitzer, 1996 - Carol Dameron - photographer*

All Photographs are copyrighted © and unless credited otherwise were taken by
Herb Snitzer and are the property of the photographer.

Creative Consultant
Bill Fogleson, Color Key Graphics

Book Design by Judy Adamski
KioCom Design Group, Inc.

Previously Published Books

The New York I Know; by Marya Mannes/Herb Snitzer; J. B. Lippincott Co.

Summerhill, A Loving World; The Macmillan Co.

Today is for Children, Numbers Can Wait; The Macmillan Co.

Reprise: The Extraordinary Revival of Early Music; by Joel Cohen/Herb Snitzer; Little Brown and Co.

To Carol Dameron
My amour and best friend,
this book is dedicated.

TABLE OF CONTENTS

Nina Simone and Herb Snitzer, backstage Town Hall, NYC, 1959, photographer unknown

INTRODUCTION

New York City, mid 20th - Century, the most dynamic of all American cities, ten years after the conclusion of WWII. The city was filled with enthusiasm, creativity, far from what we now call the conservative Dwight Eisenhower years, for they were anything but to this newly college graduated artist, moving to New York for very much the reasons why most young people move to New York; to be a part of the nerve of their generation, to become successful, perhaps even well known in their worlds, and to eventually know and become friends with many other young men and women whose ambitions paralleled their own.

Those were heady days, filled with paradox, contradiction, intellectual excitement, creative growth and music of all kinds all around me from Leonard Bernstein's New York Philharmonic and John Cage's avant-garde energies to the emerging bebop of Dizzy Gillespie and Charlie Parker. It was also what we now call the Golden Age of jazz, in that the "older" jazz players- Armstrong, Ellington, Lester Young, Red Allen, Roy Eldridge, Coleman Hawkins- were still in their prime, and the young turks were coming onto the scene - Miles Davis, Max Roach, Thelonious Monk, John Coltrane, Ornette Coleman, Nina Simone, Charles Mingus. You will meet many of them as you turn the pages of my book. Most are gone now. In their place another generation of players, and of course, a fourth generation is now the mainstream.

This book is a collection of images made over a long period of time, images of friends and strangers, for jazz musicians are forever traveling, and I have been away from New York for a long time. Some of the images were made at festivals, concerts, clubs, where the contact between me and the artists was fleeting, where little conversation took place. Other images were made of friends whom I have known for a long time, who allowed me the entre needed to make images under positive and open conditions. I am re-minded of a conversation that my friend, the great rock 'n roll photographer, Jim Marshall told me about Miles Davis. Miles was looking at Jim's photographs of John Cotrane, and he said to Jim, "Why don't you make pictures of me like you do of John?" And Jim's response was classic. "Miles, why don't you let me make pictures of you, like John does." End of problem, for Miles was known for giving photographers trouble.

In the mid 20th century, jazz was a troubling music: A music primarily made and played by a people whose ancestors were unwillingly brought to America. The pain, suffering and separation experienced by African Americans over these past 400 years, poignantly comes through in the music, music that contains all the heartbreak and pain of a people chained and cut off from their own history. These experiences are expressed in the music we call "the blues", through which jazz was born, and brought to maturity by men and women whose ancestors helped build America.

The past forty years has witnessed social and political upheaval throughout the world. Jazz has been a part of this transformation. It is no accident that blacks have been in the forefront of change. Read James Baldwin in "Go Tell It on the Mountain". "Yes, their parts were cut off, they were dishonored, their very names were nothing more than dust blown disdainfully across the field of time, to fall where, to blossom where, bringing forth what fruit hereafter, where? - Their names were not their own. Behind them was the darkness and all around them destruction, and before them nothing but the fire - A bastard people far from God, crying and singing in the wilderness."

There is a sadness to the music, never far removed from the surface, no matter how "light" the music may seem. I was drawn to the music for many reasons, but my experiences as a white, lower middle-class, and uncultured young man seemed far removed. Whether it be physical or mental slavery, slavery binds, and color is irrelevant, or so I believe. I was drawn to the paradox and dynamics of the music. I was also drawn to the people who play(ed) the music, not all terrific people, far from it. There are wonderful people and terrible people in all professions, and I met the full gamut in the jazz world. But for the most part, the men and women who make the music are decent, hard working and creative persons, interested in all that is positive about life. The anger, the hate, the love and sorrow are all elements reflected in jazz.

Jazz is the only American "art form" whose major figures and musical influences are black men and women. By definition then, I am suggesting rather forthrightly that the major contributions to the musical life of America, were and are, made by African Americans. This in no way suggests that contributions by white composers to the musical life of America should be ignored or seen as secondary. History won't allow that to happen. When I look at the music of Duke Ellington, the first among equals, the argument is concluded. No other composer can begin to be compared to Ellington, although a few critics try all the time. He simply is beyond category, not only because he was the best of all composers, but because he, also, kept an orchestra on the road for fifty years, traveling, playing, composing, doing what he had to do to keep his orchestra together. The effort alone was overwhelming. Critics nitpick about the contributions made to the Ellington "songbook" by Juan Tizol, Billy Strayhorn, Lawrence Brown, and others as "proof" that Duke wasn't all that great. Silly stuff like that keeps the jazz world humming.

For me it became specific when the editor of the magazine <u>Metronome</u>, assigned me to photograph the great tenor saxophonist, Lester Young. The glorious and mellifluous Lester Young, mainstay, for many years, of the Count Basie Orchestra, was doing a solo gig at the *Five Spot Café* in the bowery. So on a cooling October evening in 1958, Bob Perlongo, the associate editor of <u>Metronome</u> and I , traveled to the bowery, and what started out as a one night gig turned into a forty year journey, meeting and photographing jazz artists throughout the world.

Lester Young, or "Prez" as he was called, appeared through the darkness, in his sadness and melancholy, in a long black coat, his porkpie hat situated squarely on his head; his "axe" in a black leather case carried loosely by his side. He almost shuffled as he walked. That very first negative made of Lester Young is now considered by many to be the quintessential image of "Prez", and it has lasted forty years. I feel blessed, and am grateful for the acknowledgment.

Lester died six months later, March 15, 1959. From that day (night) on, jazz musicians have been part of my life. Their music, entertaining, and intellectually stimulating, and their life-styles, swingin'. No Chet Baker, no Clint Eastwood or Spike Lee films. "Straight, No Chaser", the Thelonious Monk composition, and title of a film on him is where it's at. Simple and honest, no frills, just the action and the jazz artist. So, one day, when I close my eyes and listen hard to Duke Ellington's Orchestra, I just might hear Sarah (Vaughan), Ella (Fitzgerald) and Carmen (McRae) singing a song that will last forever. Now that would be something.

As you travel with me through the pages of this book, you will meet people and read stories filled with love and caring. I hope you will come away with the feeling that terrific people make this music we call Jazz. No drum machines, no canned elevator music, and no soft jazz pabulum. Straight ahead, no games, just great music, made by great artists. Come on the journey.

Herb Snitzer
St. Petersburg, FL
November, 1999

On the bus in Connecticut, 1960

Louis Armstrong

Pops was, for me, the most caring and thoughtful of all the musicians I've known. I took a weekend bus trip with him and his band, and on that trip I made these images. He was a humane and giving person who put me at ease from the start. He loved to joke and that weekend was filled with humor, wisecracks, and some damn great music.

The Star of David? It was a gift from the Karnovsky family in New Orleans when Pops was just a child. They cared for him, fed and clothed him. He wore the Star his entire life. He was the least prejudiced musician I ever knew.

Tanglewood, MA, 1960

Nina Simone

One of my first assignments was to photograph the talented but difficult Nina Simone for an album cover. I had briefly met Nina in Philadelphia. We hit it off, found much to talk about. The photography session took many hours of hard work, but out of it came a cover and a set of images, which show Nina's early, good-natured side.

I, also, owe a special thanks to Nina Simone. She opened the jazz world to me again by asking me to photographically cover two concerts she was doing in Bern, Switzerland in December of 1986 which brought me into contact with Hans Zurbrügg, the producer of the *International Jazz Festival, Bern*. He hired me to cover his festival in 1987 and brought me back to Switzerland again in 1988 and 1989. This enabled me to reconnect with jazz friends from all over the world and to add new images to a collection that has greatly enriched and enlarged my jazz photographic archives. Thank you, Nina and Hans.

Philadelphia, PA, 1959

NINA

Philadelphia, PA, 1959

9

Newport Jazz Festival, 1990

Miles Davis

This image was made at the 1990 *Newport Jazz Festival*. Miles would be dead a year
later. Miles had just finished his set and was standing in the doorway of his dressing
room, contemplating a question from an admirer. As he was reflecting, I was quietly
making frame after frame, knowing as surely as I ever knew when an image was being
created, that I was making visual history concerning Miles Davis. Miles was an outstand-
ing musician, less so a human being. I am always reminded of Arturo Toscanini's comment regarding Richard Wagner. "As a composer I take off my hat to him. As a man, I
put it back on." Miles was always so conflicted about life; an eternal romantic, or so I
believed, who never really figured it out. So, he was continuously being hurt or betrayed.
He developed a hard surface, a macho stance as if this would protect him. Never did. He
always reminded me of a male Nina Simone and vice versa. They both could have used a
lot of loving.

Apollo Theater, Harlem, NY, 1960

Recording session, Roulette Records, NYC, 1960

Eddie Jones

Huge hands surrounding the neck of the bass. Eddie Jones was laying down the beat for the Count Basie Orchestra when I first met him in 1960. Born in Red Bank, NJ, as was Bill Basie, Eddie Jones' career both in and out of music had been steady and comfortable. Eddie became vice president of computer operations for a major insurance company. After retiring from that gig, he returned full-time to the music world. I last saw him in Switzerland, 1989, newly married, looking wonderful; always steady, a gentleman first class. He died in 1999.

EDDIE

Recording session, Roulette Records, NYC, 1960

Bill "Count" Basie

Bill was someone I never really knew, but being around him and his band was always a great thrill. The memory that stays with me was seeing Bill at Duke Ellington's funeral service in New York City's *Cathedral of St. John, the Divine*. The huge hall was filled to capacity with every famous jazz and music artist imaginable. I had arrived early, knowing there would be a crowd. During the service I turned and looked at Bill, and he was crying, uncontrollably. Just shaking. That was all it took for my own tears to flow.

Count Basie, a great artist, was a warm and caring human being. I recall with great fondness those nights at New York City's *Birdland*, Bill kicking the band to perform; yes, sometimes beyond their immeasurable greatness. But he was like that, always reaching, searching.

COUNT

Backstage Village Gate, NYC, 1961

16

John Coltrane

One of the great musical artists of the 20th Century, photographed on a hot and sultry August evening in 1961, backstage at *The Village Gate*, Art D'Lugoff's wonderful (and now gone) Greenwich Village club. The Coltrane Quintet was on a break and John was quietly reading when I made the best of all my Coltrane images. That evening at *The Gate*, in addition to John Coltrane and Eric Dolphy, The Horace Silver Quintet and Art Blakey and The Jazz Messengers were also appearing. Throughout the evening the club was half-empty. So much for the "Golden Age" and popularity of jazz. So how much was John making that evening? Five bucks? Maybe ten? Jazz was a hard life-style for a long, long time.

'TRANE

Randalls Island Jazz Festival, NYC, 1959

Jimmy Rushing

The voice of The Count Basie Orchestra for many years, the Blues belonged to Jimmy. And when he sang the world was in order. Yet sadly, one encounter stands out above all. We were at *The Virginia Beach Jazz Festival*, 1961 and Jimmy had just finished his set and was backstage, looking tired and old. I motioned him to a chair and asked him to sit down and relax. His response has never left me. "Oh, no, Herb," he said. "I don't sit when white people are present." My jaw went slack and I stared at him thinking perhaps he was "putting me on." But he was dead serious. A huge wave of sadness passed over me. The effects of segregation and Jim Crow laws were and are insidious.

New York City, 1959

Dizzy Gillespie

One of the real forces in jazz, for a long time. His influence on younger players was tremendously strong: as witness John Faddis, Wynton Marsalis, Nicholas Payton. Almost everyone taking up the trumpet has to "pass through" Roy Eldridge, Dizzy Gillespie, and of course, the king of them all, Louis Armstrong.

Dizzy was always inspirational, funny, and committed to his faith and his music. The last time I saw him he loaned me his limousine. But, this is a long story; the essence being his desire to help when needed. This was reciprocated by musicians all over the world when he put his United Nations Orchestra together. I recall asking trombonist, Slide Hampton, why he was playing in the orchestra when he could be making much more money doing his own gigs. "Because Dizzy asked me," was Slide's quiet response.

DIZZY

Hunter College, NYC, 1959

Thelonious Monk

Photographed just before he played at the United Nations in 1960. This was one of the few times Monk wore a suit; in deference to the U.N. He even took off his hat when he played — though he kept on his sunglasses.

Monk and I used to play ping-pong. I always thought I'd win a game, but I never did. He was like a cat around the table: quick, alert, always in the present. When he made music he was both in the present and somewhere else. Going deeper and higher, right into the stars.

United Nations, NYC, 1960

MONK

United Nations, NYC, 1960

23

Five Spot Cafe, NYC, 1958

Lester Young

The lights from the *Five Spot Cafe* window threw a blanket of brightness onto a graying and dirty sidewalk as we waited for a living legend to appear. Lester Young would play that October, 1958 evening to a small but dedicated audience of less than 40 people.

The "we" who waited consisted of Bob Perlongo – a staff writer for *Metronome* magazine, myself – a young photographer on his first jazz assignment and Lester's manager, whose name I cannot recall some 40 years later. *The Five Spot* was already a well-known club for the Jazz Avant Garde: Monk, Mingus, Coltrane, Eric Dolphy, Jimmy Guiffre, Cecil Taylor and Ornette Coleman all played their strange music there in those heady days of what we now consider the "Golden Era" of jazz; the years when the changeover from swing to be-bop and beyond became complete. But Lester Young was special. He was considered then – still is – one of the greatest tenor saxophonists of all time.

On a personal level, he came to symbolize much more. He gave me my first taste of this music of freedom and sparked what would become my lifelong obsession with jazz. He stepped out of the darkness dressed in a long black coat. His pork- pie hat settled squarely on his head. His saxophone nestled comfortably under his arm. Later, by the window light of the cafe, I made the first of many photographs that evening. My first negative of a jazz musician was termed by jazz critic, Nat Hentoff, "The quintessential Lester Young photograph." Later that evening, he put the instrument to his lips and transported this young photographer to places within the stars. Places from which, I knew, I would never return. Lester Young died six months later on March 15, 1959.

Jazz Boat, Boston, MA, 1982

Zoot Sims

Soon after Zoot Sims died, his widow, Louise Sims, called and asked if she could use this photograph on the cover of his memorial pamphlet. It was being produced for his church service conducted by Reverend John Gensel, the "Jazz Priest," (whom I met in 1960, when this young man with a reversed collar started hanging out in jazz clubs; but, this is another story). I told Louise she certainly could use the photograph of Zoot. This photograph eventually ended up in President Bill Clinton's collection. Zoot was one of his favorite musicians, whom he never had the good fortune to meet.

Zoot was a wonderful player. He and Al Cohn formed the Zoot Sims/Al Cohn Quintet. I spent many a night at the *Half Note Cafe* in New York City watching them trade solos and drinks through the night. Sadly, the drinking finally "did them both in." Zoot died at 59 years of age and Al, gone at 62.

ZOOT

Sarasota, FL, 1992

Dorothy Donnegan

A pianist extraordinaire; comfortable with classical music, as well as jazz and Broadway tunes. She loved to interact with her audiences while playing in a club. I recall one incident in New York City - although this image was made in Florida - where in the audience a party was taking place. Dorothy, never missing a musical beat, asked what was the occasion. She was told it was a fortieth wedding anniversary party. Whereupon, she exclaimed that she NEVER reached that number with her four husbands. This, of course, cracked up the entire audience. She was unheralded in her lifetime, yet was certainly known and appreciated by the jazz family.

DOROTHY

Newport Jazz Festival, 1959

30

Charles Mingus

One of the more talented jazz players and equally difficult, however, as a human being. Very high strung, and too often intolerant of others. Yet, in his presence one felt an energy and enthusiasm that was contagious. Powerful is how I would characterize Charles. His music and politics tied together; his loves and hates equally bound. I always stood removed from Charles. Yet I was fascinated by his person and certainly by his music. I consider him as important as any other jazz composer of the 20th Century. Only Duke Ellington and Thelonious Monk are on a higher plateau.

On the road, NYC, 1960

Trummy Young

One of the first musicians I came to know. He helped me enormously when I met and photographed Louis Armstrong. Trummy took me under his wing and guided me through the introductions. This was an important moment for me, taking a weekend bus trip with "Pops" and his band. I was quite nervous.

Trummy Young is considered one of the top three trombone players, along with Jack Teagarden and J.J. Johnson. I considered him a friend. He spent his last years living and working in Hawaii. His sound and person were always mellow.

TRUMMY

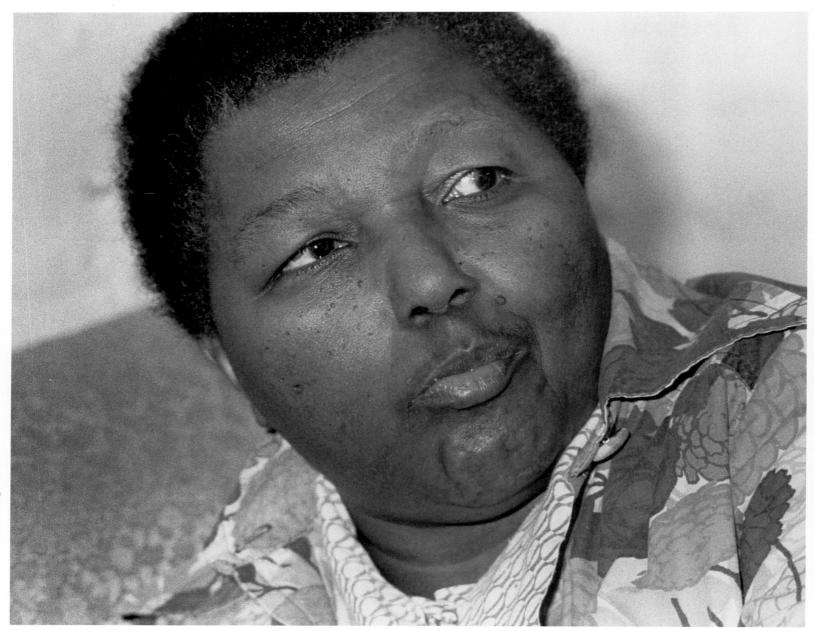

New England Conservatory, Boston, MA, 1989

Melba Liston

A rarity in the jazz world of the 40's and 50's, a female horn player. Melba was a trombone player and a damn good trombone player who was always tested by the macho men of jazz; which was (is) a masculine world especially on brass instruments. Yes, there were female jazz singers and piano players, but few brass players of any national reputation. The jazz world mirrored the larger world in women being secondary, but I always felt it was one of the few areas where the black man could feel supreme. And, so, black women had to "know their place." (What a terrible phrase). But Melba was also a composer and an arranger first class. Her combining talents with pianist Randy Weston was a breath of fresh air for them both. She died in 1999.

MELBA

New England Conservatory, Boston, MA, 1989

Randy Weston

A great talent, unheralded in his own country. I love his piano playing, and totally respect him personally. Randy spends half the year in Africa and the other half living in Brooklyn. He is a large man whose hands would be the envy of any NFL wide-receiver. They are enormous and cover half the piano keys, or so it seems to me.

I saw him last in Boston, when he and Melba Liston gave a joint concert, he playing her compositions. Randy is like so many other jazz musicians out there: receiving very little acclaim from the popular press, going his own way, an artist involved with creation, always having something to say musically.

Steve Gadd

More known as a rock, rather than a jazz drummer, Steve Gadd is respected by all other musicians because he can REALLY play, making music rather than noise. Drummer Max Roach once remarked that too many young players play a lot of notes, but they make no music. In Gadd's case, music flows continuously. I met Steve in Europe, as his band, "The Gadd Gang" was touring around. Once again, *The International Jazz Festival*, *Bern*, was the setting.

International Jazz Festival, Bern, 1989

Birdland, NYC, 1960

Jimmy Heath

Is the getup the 70's or what? Photographed at Portland High School, he was giving a workshop prior to an evening concert. Jimmy came to Portland, ME, where I was living in 1977, and was part of a year long jazz series that I had put together with Dick Colby, an Episcopal priest. A local trio would back a well known player who would do a concert and a series of workshops; the NEA working at its finest. Jimmy is a great composer, one of the very best, along with being an arranger and player. But the outfit? Classic, just classic. His evening's performance was equally so. He always liked to say that he enjoyed being with me because it wasn't often that he could look a producer straight in the eyes. (We are both 5'6" tall).

JIMMY

Randalls Island Jazz Festival, NYC, 1959

Herbie Mann
& Baba Olitunji

This image was made at the *Randalls Island Jazz Festival*,
1959. What matters is that Herbie and Baba are still alive and
still making music. Herbie is recovering from prostate cancer;
has become a spokesperson for the "war" against prostate
cancer and has enough work to live comfortably with his wife, in
Santa Fe.

I knew Baba when he used the name, Michael. Over the years,
as with so many other Africans, he took a name indigenous to a
part of Africa from where he thinks he came. His comment to
the effect that "all music starts with the beat of a drum and the
beat of a drum comes from the beat of the heart" has been basic
to my way of making a photograph. I thank him for that comment every time I make an image that "hangs on."

Portland, ME, 1977

Al Cohn

Al is one of my most favorite jazz players, both as a musician and as a human being. He was, also, one of the funniest people. He was the consummate jazz player: steady, dependable, on time, in tune, and always ready to play. Too much alcohol took him down at age 62; a real loss to me personally and to the jazz world professionally.

AL

Regatta Bar, Cambridge, MA, 1990

Ernestine Anderson

A grandmother many times over, she lives in Seattle, WA when not on the road. Ernestine is fun to be with. I met her in Cambridge, MA, and she did something many show business people do not do. She bought me dinner. I was impressed and have never forgotten the gesture. Get her CDs. She is something special - and not because of the dinner. A wonderful voice!

ERNESTINE

International Jazz Festival, Bern, 1988

Horace Silver

A prolific composer, who is respected throughout the music world. I have had little personal contact with Horace; seeing him at clubs, concerts, festivals - always from a distance. But what I have seen was a mild, even-tempered man who is loved by everyone.

Randalls Island Jazz Festival, NYC, 1959

HORACE

BB King

The great trumpet player - and longtime friend - Clark Terry once told me that, "You won't find more of a gentleman than BB King. He is simply the most gracious person I know." And coming from Clark, I was anxious to meet King after his set at the *International Jazz Festival, Bern*, 1988. We all gathered backstage and Clark made the introductions. I looked into sincere and gentle eyes. This was the only time I had the opportunity to say hello to BB King.

International Jazz Festival, Bern, 1988

BB KING

International Jazz Festival, Bern, 1988

International Jazz Festival, Bern, 1987

Buddy Guy

It was a real pleasure working with and getting to know him, albeit briefly, when I spent a weekend at his Chicago club. It was filled to capacity because he was the star attraction that particular weekend. I had previously met him at *The International Jazz Festival, Bern*, 1987, where he performed with Jr. Wells, and they sure "tore it up" that evening. I met him again in December, 1990 on assignment for Silvertone Records to photograph the cover image for Guy's CD, "Damn Right I've Got The Blues." (December 20/21 in Chicago). I was never so cold in all my life, but he and the music were warming. Out of that came a number of Guy images that I treasure to this day.

Chicago, IL, 1990

International Jazz Festival, Bern, 1987

Junior Wells

A great blues artist, recently dead. He was "somethin' else" to listen to! I met him when he and Buddy Guy played in the *International Jazz Festival, Bern*, 1987.

They received a standing ovation from the impassive Swiss audience. I never knew what a Swiss audience felt until <u>after</u> a song was finished. Weird. Very weird.

International Jazz Festival, Bern, 1987

JUNIOR

Sarasota Blues Festival, Sarasota, FL, 1992

Katie Webster

A blues legend, whom I photographed in Sarasota, FL. I've not seen her before or since, but while with her I felt her joy and concern for other musicians. That was enough for me. A fleeting moment in time, quickly gone, but for the image, which brings back that moment in time, forever. She died September, 1999, far to young.

International Jazz Festival, Bern, 1987

Scott Hamilton

A lyrical moment in Bern, Switzerland, 1987; Scott warming up. The
mural on the wall seems to come out of his horn, with the aloneness of
the musician exemplified by the hallway going back into the picture.
No one else is present; just the artist, his music and the setting. Scott,
at the time, was one of the up and coming jazz players, with many
albums (in those days) to his credit. Haven't heard much from him in
a long time.

Boston GLOBE Jazz Festival, 1990

Sonny Rollins

Still out there. Still making music. Still the best improviser in jazz today, yesterday, perhaps tomorrow, too. When not involved with his music, he is talking about environmental pollution to anyone and everyone willing to listen. He really becomes quite agitated when he speaks about government, pollution, and, sometimes, almost any other subject prior to going on stage. Lucille Rollins once told me that Sonny has to work himself up before he goes on stage, allowing the energy to, then, come through his horn. Charlie Parker once said that his life experiences came through his horn, and that if you haven't anything to say, well, that is because you haven't really lived. So much for "smooth jazz."

Newport Jazz Festival, 1990

Gerry Mulligan

A tough act, at least my experiences tell me this. I first met him in 1960 when he came backstage to see Louis Armstrong, and then I met him a few times more in New York City. But it was in 1983, when he came to Harvard University to play with Tom Everett's Harvard Jazz Band, that I saw a side of Mulligan that was simply nasty. He was rehearsing the band when he simply stopped the music and berated them in no uncertain terms; telling them they needed to play better, that they sounded like amateurs (which they were, actually) and he wouldn't tolerate sloppy playing. On and on he went. The members of the band were far from chopped liver. They were Harvard students: bright, articulate, wanting to do what Mulligan asked of them. They, musically, could not measure up. So what?

Yet, on the other hand, photographer Herman Leonard told me that Mulligan was a great guy. Go Know.

Backstage, Lewisohn Stadium, NYC, 1960

GERRY

Carmen McRae

A talented musical artist and a wonderful singer who told me this image (right) was the best ever made of her. I was overwhelmed by the comment. No doubt she had thousands of photographs during her many years in show business. To be singled out was indeed an honor. Our paths crossed often, but always fleeting; a club date here, a concert there, a festival where maybe she would be around for her set, share a few hours with other jazz musicians and then, gone. Her CD, singing to the compositions of Thelonious Monk, remains my favorite.

International Jazz Festival, Bern, 1988

CARMEN

International Jazz Festival, Bern, 1988

International Jazz Festival, Bern, 1988

Joe Williams

My favorite blues singer and one of my favorite people. Joe was
something special. He took over as the singer with the Basie orchestra
when Jimmy Rushing left. He energized the band to new musical
heights. He was, also, well liked as a man. I always enjoyed seeing
him, spending time with him. There were always great stories coming
out of our getting together. I saw him last at *The Regatta Bar* in Cambridge, MA. As always, our meeting was warm, openhearted and
relaxed. No doubt he and Sarah Vaughan are singing duets together,
joined by Bill Basie and sometimes Duke Ellington. What a loss when
Joe died.

International Jazz Festival, Bern, 1989

Art Blakey

I knew Art for thirty years, from the early album cover I did on him for
BlueNote to the last time I saw him at *The International Jazz Festival,
Bern*, 1989, where I made this and other images. He was a great leader
and great teacher, nurturing many of the young musicians who are the
stars of jazz today. To play with Art was a privilege and pleasure. If
the money was sometimes less or even nonexistent, well what the hell,
the music was hip and drivin'.

Nat Adderly, Harold Land & JJ Johnson

Three great players, integral to jazz history: Trumpeter - Nat Adderly, saxophonist - Harold Land, and the great trombonist - J.J. Johnson. It was a thrill listening to them.

NAT, HAROLD & JJ

International Jazz Festival, Bern, 1987

Museum of Modern Art, NYC, 1960

Coleman Hawkins

Known to his friends as "Bean," he was always the gentleman; always dressed in a conservatively cut suit. Bean's music never dipped into the pedestrian, never was there - to me -a boring solo. He was the consummate musician. Coupled with his inherent dignity and sense of self, Bean, always made the world a better place. This image was made at the *Museum of Modern Art*, in one of the "Jazz in the Garden" series <u>Metronome</u> Magazine produced during the summer of 1960. Bean was appearing with "Little Jazz," Roy Eldridge. That summer series brought many of the older jazz performers before a new audience in a sophisticated setting.

Newport Jazz Festival, 1959

Duke Ellington

There are no words that can describe what I feel about Duke Ellington. For me, Duke was simply the best: the best orchestra leader, the best composer, the best all around teacher, the best judge of others. He kept his orchestra alive for fifty years. They were as vibrant in 1924 as they were in 1974, the year he died. 10,000 people attended his funeral - 3000 inside *Cathedral of St. John, the Divine*; the others lining the sidewalks as his casket was brought out of the church. I was living in the Adirondack Mts. when I learned of Duke's death. I took an overnight train into New York City and made my way to the church, arriving quite early, and staying all through the service. It was very moving. Stanley Dance, author, writer, delivered a dignified eulogy. Ella Fitzgerald sang Ellington's "Solitude," and Father Norman O'Connor, Duke's friend and jazz historian, said, "Duke, we thank you. You loved us madly. We will love you madly, today, tomorrow, forever."

Columbia Recording Studio, NYC, 1961

Columbia Recording Studio, NYC, 1961

Johnny Hodges

The purest alto-saxophone player of all time. The mainstay of The Duke Ellington Orchestra from 1928 to 1951 and then again from 1955 to 1970, the year he died. No other alto saxophonist could play a ballad as well as Hodges. He was the ultimate romantic, yet he always seemed impassive, cool and detached, until the notes came rushing from his horn. I loved his music. Nicknamed Jeep, or Rabbitt, he was almost as famous as Duke himself. Duke composed "Jeep's Blues" in honor of Hodges. At Duke's funeral, as the casket was being removed from the church, Hodges' saxophone, accompanying Alice Babs singing "Heaven and Almighty God," was heard from a tape recording, bringing more tears to an already drenched crowd of people.

Paul Gonsalves

He is one of my favorite Ellington sidemen, as much for his reputation as his music. I never spoke to Gonsalves, too much in awe of all jazz musicians in those days, but I observed Paul and liked what I saw and felt. He seemed sometimes "straight ahead" and sometimes very "wacko." One incident stands out. The band was playing on Long Island and Gonsalves was late, his empty chair quite noticeable. As he hurriedly made his way to the stage, frantically getting his horn out of the case, Duke called out a tune that featured a Gonsalves solo at the break. Gonsalves was frantic, trying to get his horn together which he did at the very last moment. "Boy," I thought. "That ought to teach him to be late." But, from what I came to know, Paul was late a lot of the time. And Duke always tried to, and sometimes did, teach him a lesson. Paul became a celebrity after his 39 choruses played during the performance of "Diminuendo & Crescendo in Blue" at the 1956 *Newport Jazz Festival*. That incident put Duke Ellington's orchestra back on top of the jazz world.

PAUL

Columbia Recording Studio, NYC, 1961

A television studio, NYC, 1960

Jimmy Guiffre
& Stuart Davis

I first met him when I was a young photo editor for <u>Metronome</u> Magazine. Jimmy was on television with renown painter, Stuart Davis, and a
few other jazz musicians. The program also had a Picasso sculpture
piece which replicated Jimmy's profile, hence, the image seen here.
Stuart Davis later work was influenced by jazz and as he talked, Jimmy
played. I was thrilled to be in their presence. I had known of Davis
since I was seventeen years old. Meeting and photographing him in
1960 was simply a joy beyond words. My images of Jimmy and
Stuart remain strong to this day.

Stuart Davis, 1960

The International Jazz Festival, Bern, 1988

Milt Hinton

The grandaddy of all bass players, Milton spent 18 years beating out time for *The Cab Calloway Orchestra*. Milt is the perfect gentleman - gracious. Married to his wife, Mona, for over fifty-five years, he plays the music. She takes care of business. I first met Milt in 1959 when he was part of a Dizzy Gillespie big band. This photograph was made at *The International Jazz Festival, Bern*, 1988.

Newport Jazz Festival, 1990

Tito Puente

One of the major Latin-jazz players of this century, photographed at the 1990 *Newport Jazz Festival*. Backstage with Puente were Gerry Mulligan, Herbie Hancock and Chick Corea having a classic jazz moment of fun and spontaneity, as happens when musicians come together after not seeing each other for a long time. Jazz players are constantly travelling and festivals are one of the few times they can gather, even for only a few hours of exchanging gossip, family issues, etc.

I recently saw Tito again when he played in Tampa, FL. Carol and I took her ten year old son, Tito to meet Tito. A broad smile was on Tito Puente's face when he was introduced to Tito Dameron. They talked for a few minutes as if they were the only two people in the room. (About 300 were waiting to meet Puente after the concert). It was a glorious moment for both Titos.

TITO

International Jazz Festival, Bern, 1988

Maxine Weldon

A relatively unknown blues singer who "tore it up" at the *International Jazz Festival*, *Bern*, 1988 and believe me the Swiss are a difficult audience. They give few standing ovations. But Maxine won them over and not only did she get a standing ovation, she sang another song much to the joy of the audience. Maxine lives in L.A. She travels the world singing, quite a bit in Germany. I wish she had gotten the acclaim here in The United States that she deserves.

MAXINE

Boston, MA, 1982

George Adams

Another "unknown" jazz artist. He was someone who simply played his music, packed his sax and went on to the next gig. As one of my oldest friends, trumpeter Ted Curson once told me, he and other jazz musicians are grateful for the gigs because no one has to hire them. I recall this comment when I think of George Adams and so many other jazz musicians and other artists for that matter. In my own case, no one has to buy my work, but when they do I certainly appreciate the gesture. It keeps me in food and a roof over my head.

GEORGE

Danny Richmond

The ideal drummer for Charles Mingus, he anchored the Mingus band for over 20 years. I never met Danny, but always loved his frantic playing. I made this image when he came to Cambridge MA to play at Bob Merrill's *Upstairs at The Pudding* room. The place was packed with Harvard & MIT students and a few of us "gray haired hippies from the sixties."

DANNY

Cambridge MA, 1982

Jacksonville Jazz Festival, 1995

Chuck Mangione

One of my favorite trumpet players simply because he mentions Dizzy Gillespie as his major influence and that is good enough for me! Although now "identified" with smooth jazz, Chuck can still play serious jazz. His improvisations are still spirited... thoughtful and he always has something to say.

Chuck at home, NYC, 1988.

CHUCK

Sarasota, FL, 1992

Doc Cheatham

What a lovely person! I met him in the winter of his life when he came to Sarasota, FL to perform with fellow trumpet player, Jon Faddis. Doc was in his nineties and had been on the scene forever, or so it seemed; certainly as long as I was aware of jazz and jazz players. I had always wanted to meet Doc, and was thrilled to shake his hand. But, here again, to most people Doc Cheatham is just a name. No more or less. He wasn't the greatest of trumpet players, never made any all star balloting, or the *Jazz Hall of Fame*. He was just a steady, fun filled, positive human being who loved what he did and lasted a long time and FINALLY the critics caught up with Doc. Not the other way around. As my dearly departed artist friend, Aaron Siskind, once told me, "Herb, you just have to outlast the bastards." Wow, what a comment. Yet so true.

DOC

Boston MA, 1991

Eddie Palmieri

A dynamic evening in Boston, MA where Eddie's Orchestra and Mario Bouza and his orchestra brought out the Latin population of Boston. The dancing went on and on and on. The collective energies in that vast room could have lifted a rocket to the moon. The laughter, positive feelings and joy was somethin' else. It was also an evening where in racially separated Boston one experienced all shades of color, together, joyous, grooving to powerful music. Fleeting, but enough for me to know it is possible for all people to live and experience life in positive ways.

Cambridge, MA, 1982

Pepper Adams

Here is another highly talented, yet, almost unknown player going his own way; making his music within the small jazz world, respected by his peers. Baritone saxophone players get very little attention unless you are Gerry Mulligan or Harry Carney. But the instrument anchors the brass section and a steady sound is necessary. Pepper provided that sound for a long time. He was part of the Thelonious Monk big band during the now famous *Town Hall Concert*. This image was made in Cambridge, MA, at Harvard's *Upstairs at The Pudding*.

Bob Mover & Red Rodney at the Regatta Bar, Cambridge, MA, 1982

Red Rodney & Bob Mover

A famous and not so famous player coming together to make music... and music they made. Red Rodney, famous as the trumpet player in Charlie Parker's quintet that toured the South, passed off as a "high yellow" black, when in reality he was a young redheaded Jew who loved Parker and jazz.

When I saw Red in Boston, I asked him how things were going since the Clint Eastwood film made him "famous." "Oh Herb," he said. "I'm really tired from all the traveling and attention, but listen man. I'm loving every minute of it." And love it he should. For fame is indeed fleeting... more so it seems in the jazz world than other worlds. Red wasn't a young guy by the mid eighties, already on the jazz scene for 40 years. Yet, he was still "out there," still making music and traveling. If nothing else, I always admired a jazz musician's stamina. You had to be in good shape physically.

Sheila Jordan
& Harve Swartz

Sheila is one of my favorite people, a musician whose life experiences would blow your mind. If anyone had a tough early and middle childhood, it was Sheila. And all that pain and anguish comes out in her music. She came to jazz early on while living in Detroit, hanging out with other young men and women who loved the music. She met saxophonist Frank Foster when both were teenagers. She sang with Charlie Parker at seventeen years of age. Currently she teaches, sings when the gigs come her way. She is highly respected by the jazz family. And for me, I simply love her and have for a long time.

Not leaving Harve out of the picture, he is another always working, always busy musician whom most people have never heard of, but who makes jazz what it is today.

This image was made at Harvard. Right in the middle of their performance the fire alarm went off. Sheila, not missing a beat, began to sing in the same key as the fire alarm. It just knocked me out as we all had to leave the building for half an hour. Upon our return the two musicians simply took up the beat and the music went on.

Cambridge, MA, 1982

107

Boston GLOBE Jazz Festival, 1990

Cleo Lane

I had one opportunity to meet Cleo Lane and her husband, band leader and saxophonist, Johnny Dankworth when they played the *Boston GLOBE Jazz Festival*, in the mid eighties. Cleo can sing four octaves... no small feat. Cleo is not a young woman, yet her energy and enthusiasms belie her age. She was delightful, gracious and allowed me a lot of time in making my images. So I wanted to portray her as open, positive and embracing. I think I accomplished my task.

CLEO

Joanne Brackeen

Pianist extraordinaire, way out to some. This image came about when Joanne came to Boston. I remember her concocting a tea made from roots, herbs, and other mysterious ingredients, which she said was "healthy." Being someone who is always conscious of diet and a non meat eater, non fried foods person, I am always open to trying new things. But one taste told me that whatever was in that tea, Joanne was going to have a non sharing colleague. She told me I was missing out on something important. I thanked her for her interest in my well-being.

JOANNE

Boston GLOBE Jazz Festival, 1990

Joey Defrancesco

An organ player supreme, photographed at the *Clearwater Jazz Holi-day in Florida,* 1997. No more or less. Didn't talk to him. Never saw him again. But I like the fullness of the image which reminds me of his music, very dense and direct. An unexpected rainstorm washed out half his set, much to the disappointment of the 10,000 spectators.

Clearwater Jazz Holiday, 1997

Woody Herman

He died broke and if it wasn't for Frank Sinatra, would have had no money at all in his later years. Bad management? Bad investments? Bad advice? A terrible way to go out, especially since he had such swingin' orchestras that brought great pleasure to so many hundreds of thousands of people. Woody Herman's "Herds" were famous, with many of his players going on to individual fame: Stan Getz, Jimmy Guiffre, A1 Cohn, Zoot Sims, just to name saxophone players.

Woody seemed like a nice person. I knew him early on in my career. I then met him again over 20 years later at a private party in Beverly, MA where he was playing a concert gig. He seemed tired and my image caught an unguarded moment, the best kind of image, no smiles, just a human gesture that reveals.

Beverly, MA, 1983

115

Jacksonville Jazz Festival, 1995

David Sanborn

I briefly met Sanborn when he came to my 1990 Los Angeles jazz exhibition at the Verve Gallery. Bill Goldberg, the owner of Verve, went all out and about 600 people showed up for the opening including other jazz musicians, a couple of the L.A. Lakers and dozens of aspiring Hollywood movie people. It was quite a night.

This image was made at the 1995 *Jacksonville Jazz Festival*. I didn't get the opportunity to meet or talk with Sanborn that evening, with security not believing that I knew David. So different from the "old days" when you simply knocked on the dressing room door and you were invited in. Today, with too many photographers and way too many beefed up security people, it's just not worth the effort anymore.

DAVID

Bucky Pizzarelli

"Oh, are you John's dad?" asked with humor and a twinkle in his eye. Bucky is certainly proud of his son, but Bucky is a wonderful musician in his own right, going back to big band days. I met Bucky when he was recording for Arbors Records - a jazz record company located in Clearwater, FL - featuring the piano playing of John Bunch and bassist Bob Haggart laying down the time. Now these three gentlemen exemplify all that is good and decent about jazz players. Respectful of each other and towards me as well - they are all professional in their approach to the music and to the recording session. Sadly, Bob Haggart is no longer alive, but Bucky and John continue to make wonderful music. And yes, Bucky is John's dad, much to John's good fortune.

Bradenton, FL, 1996

Newport Beach, CA, 1997

Jackie Coon,
Eddie Anderson & Me

Photographed in Newport Beach, CA during a Jackie Coon recording session by Arbors Records. Eddie, Jackie and I - were living out of our suitcases, temporarily housed in a motel conveniently located next to the recording studio. As a young man, Jackie Coon played with Jack Teagarden and can be heard on a Teagarden CD recorded live at the now long gone San Francisco, CA. *Club Hangover* in 1954. Jackie is still out there, making music. It was an honor to be with them.

International Jazz Festival, Bern, 1989

Michel Camilo

Pianist Michel Camilo and Herb Snitzer, Bern, Switzerland 1989. Conservatory trained, Michel is Dominican born, and his music is hot and fast. He is technically superb and emotionally exciting to watch. On top of all this he is a beautiful cat, open and caring. I last saw him when he played the Clearwater (FL) Jazz Holiday a few years back.

MICHEL

ACKNOWLEDGMENTS

Lots of thank yous are in order here: Many people who have believed in me and my work need to be recognized for their support and friendship.

Lee Tanner and Jim Marshall, west coast based photographers and friends for more years than we care to admit.

Peter Golenbock and Rhonda Sonnenberg, friends and exceptional writers and respected authors, collaborators on other projects.

Joe and Judy Adamski and Bill Fogleson, colleagues and unwavering supporters.

Ed and Gail Snitzer for their belief in this project.

So many others; "Doc" Sidman, Bill Goldberg, Rich Walwood, Dave Pributsky, Lennie Bennett, Tim Kennedy, Cynthia Sesso, Dave Scheiber, Nick Lagos and WMNF- FM, Greg Mussleman, David Karlak, Burton and Ellen Hersh, Tom Gessler, Rob Davidson, Reggie and Mendee Ligon, Mary Jane Dameron, Brad and Susan Wendkos, Chuck Levin, John Sandhaus, Allen Weinberg, Eva, Tito and Teopolo Dameron, Ron Sampson, my children; Lisa Snitzer, Susie Renner, Sigrid Ann, Werner Snitzer and Laura Zatta. I would be remiss in not mentioning my grandchildren; Sasha Rescorl, Ian and Zoe Renner and my son-in-law, Peter Rescorl.

Gus Kayafas, publisher of my portfolio, <u>Such Sweet Thunder.</u>

A special thanks to photographer, Rodger Kingston for insisting that I go back into my jazz files and print the classic images of Louis Armstrong, Duke Ellington, John Coltrane, Sarah Vaughan and so many others.

And lastly, an enormous thanks to all jazz musicians throughout the world!